THE NATURE KIDS GUIDE TO

CAPYBARAS

DAVID ANDERSON

LP Media Inc. Publishing
Text copyright © 2026 by LP Media Inc.
All rights reserved.

For information address LP Media Inc. Publishing,
30012 Variolite St NW, Princeton MN 55371
www.lpmedia.org

Publication Data

Capybaras
The Nature Kid's Guide to Capybaras — First edition.

Summary: "Learn all about Capybaras, the Nature Kid Way"
— Provided by publisher.

ISBN: 979-8-89818-105-5

[1. Capybaras – Non-Fiction] I. Title.

Title: The Nature Kid's Guide to Capybaras

CONTENTS

WETLAND WONDERS

Squeak! A capybara sits in shallow water. Its nose pokes above the surface.

Capybaras are the largest rodents in the world. They are only found in South America, where they need water to survive.

Capybaras make their homes near **wetlands**. They live by rivers, ponds, and marshes. Tall grasses grow along the water's edge, giving them places to hide.

Water keeps capybaras cool in hot weather. It also helps them stay safe from danger. This is why they spend much of their time near the shore.

Wetlands give capybaras everything they need. They find food, water, and shelter all in one place.

SOUTH AMERICAN STARS

Rustle! A capybara walks through tall grass near a riverbank.

Capybaras live in most of South America. You can find them in Brazil, Venezuela, and Colombia.

They live from Panama all the way to Argentina. They like warm places where it never gets too cold. Cold weather is hard for them.

Some capybaras live in grasslands. Others live in rainforests. But they always stay close to water.

Capybaras have webbed feet like ducks. This makes them great swimmers!

GIANT RODENTS

Thump! A capybara stands next to a dog. This rodent is much bigger!

Capybaras are giant **rodents**. They can weigh up to 140 pounds. That is as heavy as a large dog.

These animals grow about two feet tall. They can be four feet long from nose to tail. They are relatives of guinea pigs.

Guinea pigs weigh only two pounds. That means capybaras are about 70 times heavier. They are truly giant versions of their small cousins.

A capybara's head alone can be as long as a whole guinea pig's body is from nose to tail.

BUILT TO SWIM

Splash! A capybara dives into a pond. Its body glides smoothly.

Capybaras have bodies made for swimming. Their **webbed feet** push through water like paddles. This helps them move fast in rivers and ponds.

Their eyes, ears, and nostrils sit on top of their heads. This lets them see, hear, and breathe while mostly underwater. Only a small part of their face shows above the surface.

Capybaras have barrel-shaped bodies with short, strong legs. Their coarse fur also helps in the water. It dries quickly when they leave.

SNIFF IT
OUT

Sniff! A capybara lifts its head. It smells the air.

Capybaras have a strong sense of smell. They use their noses to find food. They can also smell danger nearby.

Their hearing is very good too. Capybaras have small ears that sit high on their heads. They can hear predators before they see them.

Capybaras rely on their strong hearing and smell to stay safe.

Capybaras have scent glands on their noses to mark territory.

HIDE AND BLEND

Whoosh! A capybara stands perfectly still in the brown grass.

Capybaras have brown fur. This color matches dry grass and mud, so **predators** have a hard time spotting them.

These animals stay very still when danger is near. They crouch low to the ground. Their eyes and ears sit on top of their heads. This helps them hide in water while still watching for danger.

Capybaras also hide in thick plants near water.

A capybara's brown fur changes shade with the seasons, darker when wet.

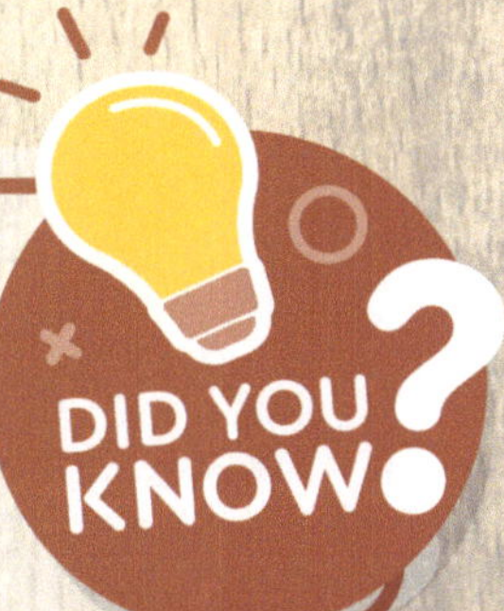

GRASS GRAZERS

Chomp! A capybara bites off a big mouthful of grass.

Capybaras eat mostly grass. They spend many hours each day **grazing**. Their large front teeth never stop growing, but chewing tough grass wears the teeth down.

Capybaras also eat water plants. They munch on reeds and lilies in ponds. Sometimes they eat bark and soft fruits too.

These animals eat a lot each day. An adult can eat six to eight pounds of plants.

Capybaras eat their own droppings for vitamins. Gross but healthy!

CAPYBARA CHATTER

Capybaras can make a sound like a dog's bark to warn others of predators.

Click! Click! A capybara calls to its group.

Capybaras make many sounds. They click, whistle, and bark. Each sound has a meaning. A mother clicks to call her babies. A loud bark means danger is near.

Capybaras also purr. They make this soft sound when they feel calm. You might hear purring when capybaras rest together in water.

Baby capybaras are very vocal. They make high squeaking sounds. These squeaks help mothers find their young. Capybaras can even talk while swimming. They keep their noses above water to call out.

DANGER LURKS

Growl! A jaguar crouches near the water. A capybara looks up.

Capybaras have many predators. Jaguars hunt them on land. These big cats wait near water to catch capybaras.

Caimans also eat capybaras. These reptiles grab them from below the water. Anacondas are another danger in the water.

In the sky, large birds watch for baby capybaras. Harpy eagles can swoop down fast. Vultures hunt young ones too.

On land, pumas and ocelots also hunt capybaras in some areas.

SPLASH AND DASH

Swoosh! A capybara races toward the river. It leaps in!

Capybaras have a quick escape plan. When they sense danger, they run straight for water. Once there, they can hold their breath for up to five minutes.

These animals hide under the surface. Only their eyes, ears, and nose peek above the water. This helps them breathe while staying hidden.

Capybaras also bark loudly to warn others.

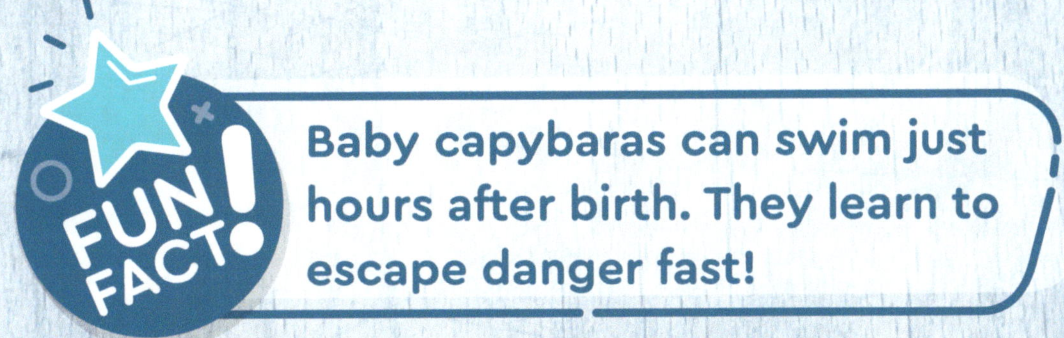

SUPER SWIMMERS

Grunt! A capybara paddles across a lake. Its nose pokes above water.

Capybaras are excellent swimmers. They move through water with ease. Their webbed feet push them forward like paddles.

These animals swim almost every day. They cross rivers and lakes to find food. They also swim to cool off.

Capybaras can swim fast when needed. Their eyes stay above water as they go.

Capybaras can close their ears and nostrils underwater. Special flaps keep water out.

CHILL DAYS

Snort! A capybara yawns in the warm sun. It stretches on the riverbank.

Capybaras spend a lot of time resting. They often lie in mud or shallow water. This keeps them cool during hot days.

These animals are most active in the morning and evening. They use cooler hours to eat. At midday, they rest in groups.

Capybaras also groom each other. They use their teeth to clean fur gently.

Capybaras often rest in piles of up to 20 animals. Younger ones climb on top of adults like living pillows!

CAPY
CREWS

Chirp! A group of capybaras rests close together by the water.

Capybaras live in groups. A group can have ten to twenty animals. They stay close together most of the time.

Each group has one main male. Several females and young ones live with him. Some groups also have other males.

Living together helps capybaras stay safe. With more eyes watching, they can spot predators faster.

When one capybara spots danger, the whole group listens. A single bark sends everyone rushing to the water together.

FINDING LOVE

Sniff! A male capybara sniffs the air. A female walks nearby.

Capybaras can have babies at any time of year. But most births happen during the rainy season, when more food grows.

The main male in a group mates with females. Other males may try too. About five months later, females give birth.

Capybaras often mate in water. This helps females escape from males they do not like.

Female capybaras can have one to eight babies at a time. Most litters have four pups.

32

Squeek! A tiny capybara pup follows its mother through the tall grass.

Baby capybaras are called pups. A mother can have one to eight pups at a time. Most litters have about four babies.

Newborn pups can walk and swim right away. They are born ready to go, with fur, open eyes, and a weight of about three pounds.

Pups start eating grass within a week. But they also drink milk for several months. Young capybaras grow quickly during their first year.

Capybara pups can run fast enough to keep up with adults just hours after birth. They swim on day one!

GROUP GUARDIANS

Bark! An adult capybara stands guard while pups play nearby.

Capybara mothers share the work. Any female in the group can nurse any pup. This helps all the babies get enough milk.

Adults take turns watching for danger. While pups play or rest, grown capybaras stay alert.

Pups learn by copying adults. They watch how to find food and swim. Young capybaras stay with their group for about a year before going off on their own.

A nursing female may feed up to twelve pups that are not her own.

ESCAPE ROUTES

Capybaras can sleep in water. They rest with their nose poking out so they can breathe while they nap safely.

Splash! A capybara dives into the water to hide.

Capybaras have special ways to stay safe. They live in groups of 10 to 20 members. Many eyes watch for danger together, and one loud bark warns the whole group.

Water is their best escape. They can hold their breath for up to five minutes. They hide underwater with just their eyes, ears, and nose poking above the surface – like a furry periscope!

Their brown fur helps them blend into muddy riverbanks. When they stay perfectly still, predators have a hard time spotting them among the reeds and shadows.

CAPYBARA SPOTTING

Splash! A capybara swims across a calm river.

Capybaras only live near rivers, lakes, and wetlands in South America. If your family ever visits places like Brazil or Venezuela, you might spot them from boats or along riverbanks.

But you can see capybaras at many zoos in closer to home. Some zoos even let you feed them or watch them swim! The best time to watch is early morning when they're most active.

Capybaras are calm animals. They don't mind being watched and often relax right in front of zoo visitors. They're one of the friendliest animals you'll ever see!

GLOSSARY

rodents
Animals with large front teeth that never stop growing, like mice and squirrels.

wetlands
Places where water covers the ground, like swamps and marshes.

predators
Animals that hunt and eat other animals.

webbed feet
Feet with skin between the toes that help animals swim.

grazing
Eating grass and plants that grow on the ground.